Poems

A Journey of the Mind

Clarence Walsh

NICJERMAIN PUBLISHER— Bronx, New York
Paperback ISBN: 979-8-9862962-0-3
Hardcover ISBN: 979-8-9862962-1-0
eBook ISBN: 979-8-9862962-2-7
Library of Congress Control Number: 2022909751
Title: Poems: A Journey of the Mind
Author: Clarence Walsh
Digital distribution | 2022
Paperback | 2022
Hardcover | 2022

Acknowledgment

I hope the readers will encounter humor in some of the composition in its verse, as Deborah Payne, who interrupts me on many occasions while I am in my profound thoughts, hunting words of substance, requesting of me to read my imaginary narratives to her. There were several of my poems she found deep humor in that would make her crack-up. There is a featured poem in the book that I assume resonates with her personally. She always requests of me to read, "Secret". DEBORAH, I appreciate your kind words of encouragement to pursue my idle time engagement into an inspirational passion. Thank you!

My sincere thanks and appreciation to my son, Patrick Walsh who has always been haunting me to publish my works of writing.

Deep and sincere thanks to Ricarda Schubmann (Rica) "baby get your poems published," love you.

Tanya always asking me to read my poems while we are on the phone. Tanya Russell, thanks for the encouragement and assisting in proofreading, and editing to publish my manuscript.

Sincere thanks to Bridget Brown.

Profound gratitude to Owen.

Preface

The letters of the alphabet form words while words create sentences. Sentences can be decisive and intrusive but not always intuitive. Sentences complete in its context inspires in various ways, creates a feeling in a person, fills you with the urge or ability to do or feel something which transforms or transcends the mind. Projecting light in a dark space even your very soul, the spiritual element of a person. Poems can unceremoniously change a person's moral or emotional nature with a level of intellectual energy and integrity. Don't be surprised when its contents in its context pierce your stone heart. Profound verses from these inspiring and uplifting verse forms intend to resurrect a spirit from its dark cloud to see the light.

The collection of literal compositions in verse that feature in this book are typically concerned with various expressions of feelings associated with the imaginative descriptions that captivate my searching mind. Poesy is regarded as qualities of beauty and emotional intensity. The nature of poetry is the physical world in a description of natural works of art that inspires the mind to evolve to undergo an evolution. But the evolution also depends on the poet's state of mind and temperament to transform a delusory scenery from the mind on to a page in collective words. The intention is to captivate the reader's mind of which the inherent qualities or characteristics are of an abstract work of art. These abstractors of the mind can have various characteristics such as achieving effects through colors, shapes, landscapes, the peaceful ocean, and the spike mountains. Then there are moods of emotion involving profound feelings and love that drift you into reality.

The delusion of the mind transcends a written summary attempting to represent a recognizable reality.

I am passionate and in a state of inner peace. The freedom from disturbance which produce, tranquility. At times in my dark and lonely moments I reach into my thoughts to find comfort in words. I hope the readers who are craving to satisfy their lust for inspiring verses will find comfort and peace of the translations of my thoughts. Each word was like fish I waited to catch at the pond of peaceful water. At times, I patiently waited for the fish to bite the bait. Slowly, with patience, the delicate words form sentences that expose in my mind. Words that form beautiful verses divulging abstracts of the mind. My silent mind does become inquisitive, wandering, taking me to places my feet have never touched and my eyes have never seen. Tranquil in thoughts from the sound of silent moments rich with emotions. Emotion always reflects stories. I hope my emotion will reflect a scenario of your stories. We all have narratives that are lost in our subconsciousness waiting to regenerate and resonate with a soothing smile that brings joy to the heart. Enjoy the beauty of creation, stand in awe of nature and wilderness. Take a glimpse of humanity in its variances. The unproductiveness of man. Will we ever understand life?

Life is a mandate with mystery! Even so death is reality. It is inevitable in life. So live life in its spring. Poems are precious gems of insights and thoughts that stay in the mind and becomes treasures in the heart. The righteous heart searches and finds "The Truth".

There is only one perfection, perfection is in its beauty. "Every good and perfect gift is from the Father above, coming down from the Father of the heavenly lights".   (James1:17)

Table of Contents

Beauty Creation 1
Life is a Garden.. 2
Love Is Strange 3
Man in the Mirror 4
Lonesome in the Land.. 5
Man of Distinction 7
Water... 8
Conception 9
Secrets...10
Laughter...11
I Am Still Holding On 12
Colors..13
Courage..15
Death...16
Deception..18
Desire 20
Eyeful..22
Dreams...24
Fate...26
Feelings..27
Fire 29
Friendship 30
Hypocrites...31
Back To Mi Roots..32
Back To My Roots..34
Heaven 36
How Could It Be 37
The Vital Map..38
Who Am I?..40
Sea...42
Home...44
Faces 45
Wild Flower 46

I Felt Your Pain..48
The Tongue 50
The Virtue Woman 52
The Spirit of Christmas...54
The Old Man 55
Summer Pleasure 57
Stillness...59
Smoke 60
Tears..61
The Cyprian 62
The Eyes..63
Time 64
Sky 66
The Power of Love..67
What Is This Life 68
Sadness with Laughter 69
Tomorrow 70

Beauty Creation

What is beauty?
It's god's creation
Beauty is diversity, it's the spectrum visualization of each being
Beauty, is the spectrum of the mind
Beauty, is the long walks digesting the outreach of the high hills and settled mountains
Beauty, it's god's creation
what is beauty?
Beauty, is the green grass, the trimmed hedges and the shady trees
Beauty, is the morning dew melting on the array of petals and buds
Beauty, it's god's creation
What is beauty?
Beauty, is the wide-open ocean with its waves beating against the white sand
Beauty, is the ship sailing in its wide-open path to its unknown destination
Beauty it's god's creation
What is beauty?

Beauty, is the birds fluttering their wings, making sweet harmonic sounds
Beauty is the silhouette sunset below the high mountains and above the wide blue sea
Beauty, it's god's creation
What is god's creation?
The moon, the stars, the heaven and earth
The dwelling beings, the plants that have their own unique purposes
Beauty, is the spectrum visualization of each being

Life is a Garden

Life is like a garden
Cultivated with various plants
Each plant is an individual
Has its own unique purpose
As agriculturist we expect
Great rewards from the sowed seeds
The rewards are not always to our expectation
We envision an excellent crop
Long plant's life span
But for some unforeseen reasons beyond our control
The harvest was not fruitful
The plants never mature to its life expectant
Though it received excellent nutrient
In life we are the plants
Cultivated in earth's-garden
As individuals with our own
Unique purpose, dreams, and expectations
Sometimes our dreams never blossom
Reality never takes its toll
Sometimes we never mature to our life span
At times we have done our uttermost best
Giving life our ultimate abilities
But we never achieve life's goals
We run a race each day
Our desire is to claim the ultimate prize
Unfortunately, we can't all win the race
No one knows what life will offer
Life is an unpredictable road

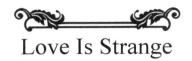

Love Is Strange

L onely, alone with the clouds
Illusive, I am not, existing in my solitary moment
Along the way green trees laugh at me
From below beautiful wild flowers happily peek up at me
Staring at me are the strokes of vibrant colors that smears the canvas
Love is strange, I looked around and the sentiments were everywhere
On skateboards, he took her hand, hand in hand and rode the clouds
Leaving the moon and stars projecting light from afar
With the aid of nature's light, it wasn't surprising to see that I was alone
Happy couples stroll by savoring the moonlight glow
Unreluctantly, they glance at the lonesome man
Strangely, the lonesome man knew all about walking hand in hand
Chasing the moonlight, both wishing on the falling star
Love is strange as tomorrow leaves footnotes of yesterday
Moments change and so does the heart
I will treasure the void in my heart
While I continue to chase the moon and stars, wishing on a falling star
I watched the bird stand alone on a fence post
I realized I am no different from a dove mourning for love
Unnoticed, that my eyes boil tears and my eyelids gushed out water
The creation has its seasons
Love is strange rotating through its season
Realized I, loneliness is self-illusion
How can I be lonesome when I have breath, breathing the source of life
I dwell in a world clustered with lively vegetation
Flying creatures that stop by, echoing sweet sounds to the ears as lullaby
Domestic animals that are delightful to stroke
Love is strange, loneliness is an illusion
It's for me to correct the misconception of my state of mind

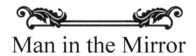

Man in the Mirror

At the mirror I met a man
His visage I hardly recognized
I assured, memory slips
With bifocal lenses, I magnified my eyes
His hair was clustered with white
Telltales from his cured countenance
… Seems he was a handsome man
The blueprint outlines do not lie
Even though he shows signs of decline
His body structure was towered and fortified
In retrospect, he was a sight to behold
Lost was the keen edge of youth
I smiled at him
Simultaneously, he acknowledged me with a smile
I thought, how pleasant was the moment
Then I perceived, we should share our thoughts
There, I pondered for questions
Will I get answers?
What does it matter?
Years gone, bye … time goes on
We wait by, in time, we wither like green grass
We transform with the eclipse of time
There was an image in the mirror
I asked, who is that man in the mirror?

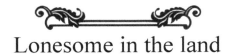

Lonesome in the land

I look to the moon and stars
When I look to the divine elements
I do not forget to look to the sun
With the glares from the sun I can see
to find my way through this lonesome land
Without a guiding helping hand
In my dark and narrow way
I look to the moon and stars
for a helping hand to guide my path
How many times I have looked for a helping hand?
But all I have seen are the divine elements
There is no coincidence looking at the three bright elements
The moon, the stars, and the sun
Their purpose is guidance for us
Through this dark and lonesome land
Day by day, night by night,
I search hoping to find another lonely soul
With candor, uprightness, and integrity
Honoring and living the just ethics of life
Cultivating the fruits of goodness
Where are the former days?
When men hold high esteem to brotherly love

Where is the neighborly watch? I am my neighbor's eyes
The deceptive attitudes of my fellow men deprive my feelings
My heavy heart is benumbed by grief
Why do men birth evil in their hearts?
There is no love for truth and peace
Who is going to heal this corrupt land?
That I can once again find an honest soul in the land
That we can communicate and hold hands
Just like the former days when men discern
each heart from their thoughts
I am lonely living in a world where I cannot trust my fellow men
With such selfishness emanating the land
I have no choice but to become a recluse in my own land

Man of Distinction

I am a man of distinction
Born of low degree, but apt to high standards
Live to serve and honor
Give honor and demand respect
Love justice, peace, and honesty
While many say I am pretentious
Will die for liberty and free will
Let it be known that there is no pride in survival
I strive for knowledge not for riches
Greed infests and destroy
I opt not for prominence or status
Corruption decomposes the core of the soul
Truth characterizes a man with uprightness and purity
There is no provocation of conscience in honesty
There is no respect of persons in fair justice
Love suppresses hate, live for charity
Peace is communication, let's abide in peace
Out of many we are one, let's live like kinsmen
Let us grow together in unity
Life is just an ephemeral span, let's live to its full potential
Let us teach and learn from each one
Let's seek to find the ultimate answer to life's mystery ...
> Wisdom

WATER - H2O

Water, the sea, the river, the lake
Water, the pond, the creek, the stream
Transparent gem
Tasteless liquid
Water, the showers that water the earth
The beaded drops of moisture
Substance of rain
Water, it tranquilizes, it calms,
It relaxes, it's serene
Water, the pearl drops, from the eyes
Water, the tears that moist the eyes
What more purifies?
Water - H2O
Such yielding characteristics
Water, it gently, quietly flows
Water, quenches, it cleanses
Water, uniquely solidifies
Statements of infinite qualities
An essence to each and everyone's
resource
Water a vital mineral of life
Aquarium, Aquarius, Aquatic
Water - H2O

CONCEPTION

HE has risen – HE has risen
Beautiful Lilies adorn the universe
It's Easter Sunday, memorialize His Resurrection
Unto me this Easter Sunday a babe is born
I sat and waited patiently
While the mother labored in travail
I thought what the little bundle will be
Pink bonnet or blue booties
For some unknown reason
The little bundle decides
Not to arrive on schedule
To ease his mother's agony of travail
The doctor on duty, decides to intervene
At six o'clock, Easter Sunday
The little bundle arrived
Twinkling ten miniature toes
He cried, inhaling his first breathe
Waiting for his little feet to be covered with little blue booties
The doctor on duty gave me a call
He said you are the father of a little baby boy
The little bundle was a boy
A son for a proud papa, dad
A mother's agony of travail
Turned into a mother's Easter Sunday bliss
My son – He was fragile and beautiful
As the Easter Lilies

Secrets

He got his - she has hers
You have yours, even I got mine
We all possessed it —SECRETS
We all have secrets
I got a secret which I will not tell
Why? Because it's a secret
Secrets are gossip
Secrets are intrusion
Secrets are personal
Many keep long dark secrets
That never been divulged
Secrets are like precious gems
Deeply embedded and locked away
Safely secured from curious ears
Some entrust their secrets
To a trustworthy confidant
While others are sworn to secrecy
Fear initiates secrets
Avoiding embarrassing moments
Protecting criminal acts
Planning surprises
Secrets refrained from the lips
Tale bearers reveal secrets
He that sworn to his secrets
Concealed the matter
Secrets are like treasures
As the whirlwind passes
So is the revelation of a secret
Who can I entrust to protect my secrets?
My tongue conceals my secrets
My secrets are safely protected with me

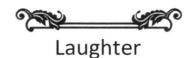

Laughter

Why do you laugh? I haven't a clue
I laugh because I am happy
I laugh because I saw something hilariously funny
Which I thought was silly you
Surprisingly I laugh when I am blue
Laughter is an antidote for my weary blues
Laughter soothes my deepest pain
It's not unusual to see me laughing up my sleeve
But surely, I am far from crazy
When I was a child, I laughed without a reason
Now I laugh for so many reasons
Going through each season
Once I had a funny experience
Leaving the dentist office
I could not contain my laughter
I was dosed with nitrous oxide, known as n2o
I was so ridiculous I became the laughingstock
All I heard was ah - ah coming from the flock
have you ever had happy tears
I have laughed to teary eyes
I have observed others laughing
Sharing happy pleasant moments
That makes my heart laugh for joy
I don't know why you laugh
But I know why I laugh
Laughter is joy, happiness, and serenity
Laughter is medicine for the soul
My heart is full with laughter

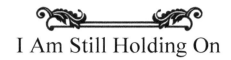

I Am Still Holding On

I am still holding on
I stand six feet tall
Having a purpose
Even though I may
not attain my dreams
I am still holding on
I climb rocky-mountains
Each God given day
My roads are long and weary
With no end in sight each day
I am still holding on
Why is my burden so heavy
Is it ethical being prejudice?
Am I in the wrong land
I am still holding on
They say I don't belong here
But my forefathers
Gave me the rights
They have paid the ultimate price
By building bridges and tunnels
In every state in sight
I am still holding on
I am stared at, I am spitted at
I have been laughed at
The name-callings are numerous
They are all out of character
But I digest them each day
I am still holding on
When will I Truly inherit
the rights of a human being?
All I demand are my respect and dignity
I will not be intimidated
Or surrender my dignity
To selfish, callus, ignorant
Self-centered human beings

COLORS

There is something fascinating about rainbows
It always captivates the eyes that beholds it
I always wondered what is so intriguing about the rainbow
Is it the spectrum of its colors that grace the blue sky?
The sun not intentionally viewed emits a cascade of brilliant colors
In a glimpse of the high sun, brilliant colors of rays shine through
the darkness reflecting waves of light
Colors are intriguing and fascinating
Colors can blow your mind
Colors will dance with your eyes
The variations of colors are numerous
Colors are diversified
There are strong colors, there are weak colors
Bright colors, faded colors
Red, black, brown, white, blue, they are all colors
You can mix colors to create new colors
What life would be without colors?
Look around, all you see is colors
Colors adorn the universe
Everything around us is affixed with colors
Rainbows, butterflies and autumn leaves

Imagine living in a world without colors
A life without beauty
In autumn the trees fascinate us with foliage of colors
When the chlorophyll fades away
The light reflects rays of colors
The flowers bloom in colors
We are defined by color
Colors differentiate, diacritically adds character
What makes the butterflies so attractive?
A variation of colors
Colors are beautiful
Beautiful, are the kaleidoscope for its colors
Appreciative, we are for eye receptors
For the variation of colors
We all have our favorite colors
What is your favorite color?

Courage

I saw the hill, oh what a tremendous sight
Compared to its strenuous mountain height
How could I get to such a great height
I heard a voice within recite
Faith, courage, and determination you must put in sight
I wondered, what about skill, strength, and might
How long would I take to climb that peaky point
I looked and looked but no courage was in sight
I searched and searched but there was no determination in my bowel
Now I hope not to lose faith
Without faith, courage, and determination are naught
Hope is always close to my heart
Gracefully, I hold on to hope
I found the strength to find faith
You cannot hope for something you possess
Then I realized I had lost faith
Then I remembered the power of believe
Belief can move great mountains
Then I started to believe again
Which I realized believing is the power of faith
With renewed faith, I found courage
With determination I stood up tall
With courage I lifted my foot and made the first crawl
Amazingly, it did not take me long
To see the beautiful footprint on the great mountain peak

DEATH

There is one thing everyone will experience
But they can never, ever relate the experience
{Death}, I have never been there
But we all know it is the definitive breath of life
We stop living and become extinct
But for sure, through our journey in life it is inevitable
No being will escape that final exhalation
Utter the word and it strikes fear
Many supplant the word death in its used
To extract the distress of its context
Many will disassociate themselves on the subject matter
Many have resistance with the thought of death
While many exhibit the mode that death will pass them by
We are all mortals which we are subject to death
It is manifested that death is imminent
There is no prejudice in death or preference
Death waits on no man's terms
Death can be slow with agony and pain
Yet, it can be like a fast jab
Coming from nowhere in split seconds
Even faster than the blink of the eyes
Strange it may be, but I am intrigued about death

Why? I know the phenomenal is sure
So why shouldn't I be self-conscious
Of the final heart strobe of life
I went to sleep and perpetually got lost in a dream
No more in sight to the eyes
Only in thoughts with memories
Accept the inevitable and be comfortable with death
Think of it, in reality, when death strikes, we missed naught
Loved ones may be left in grief but only for a spell
So, let's prepare with a clean soul for the other dimension
Available I will be, when the imminent strikes
Should it be now, tomorrow, or then
It doesn't matter when, my waiting heart prepares

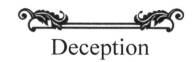

Deception

*W*hat do I hear?
I hear sounds, distant sounds
Is there deception to my ear?
Am I in a state of impairment?
Is my hearing in tune with my decibel?
What do I see?
I see looming reflections
I see shadows of silhouette images
Is it that my sight is failing?
Is there deception to my mental vision?
What do I smell?
I smell - naught, cipher
Could it be the faculty of my senses are impaired?
Is the internal orifice of my nostrils obstructed?
Are the organs of my smell in deception?
What do I hear?
I hear nuance sounds, sweet and delicate
I hear chirping, chirpy sounds that harmonize the ear
Yes, my hearing is in tune with my decibel
What do I see?
I see yellow- bellied cuckoos, chirping sparrows and
butterflies
I see a sanctuary of amphibians
I see white tailed deer, black bears and turkeys - fauna
I see a canopy of green oak trees, shading the
huckleberry and blackberry shrubs - flora
I see a conservancy of trees and lakes
There is no deception to my mental vision

What do I smell?
I smell the aroma of fresh redolent mountain air
I smell the fragrance from the fresh green grass
I smell peculiar charms bursting from the green budded
oak trees
Recumbent- reminiscing in a natural forested habitat
There is no deception to the faculties of my senses

Desire

*A*morously, from a distance he askance her
   The mirror reflects the evocative of her natural beauty
   Transparently, the eyes that behold her countenance
Would lust for such a rare natural gem
From his distance his nostrils were saturated
With the residue of her accented fragrant
The ambience was a garden
Of spicy fruits mingled with wild flowers
She was provocative, seductive, and exotic
Her skin was fresh, cool, and refined
The radiance from her un-blemished skin
Would certainly captivate any eyes
She is instinctively the self-assured woman
Sensuously, warm, luminous and feminine
Naturally, elegant with complete confidence
With a mirrored view, glancing at her subject
She carefully and gently lifts and separates
The silky filament of her lustrous hair
She gently teases her fluffy golden locks
Teasing she has grown to execute best
He was reflecting on her inward beauty
Out of many he got the chance of every man's desire
To communicate with her fragile heart
But had promised never to shatter her delicate heart
Who would overload such a caring heart
But she knew it's only a matter of time
He would break her painful heart
She as always asked why she trusts him
With such a precious commodity as her tender heart
He tries not to resist the throbbing of his lustful heart
But how long can he control his manly wants
He knew more than anyone else her sexual appetite

She knew it wouldn't be long before she succumbs to his wants
Hoping for once he would submit and halt being recalcitrant
Suddenly, she was overcome with a boiling sensation
Perspiration was emanating beyond control
Sporadically hot flashes were taking its toll
Dank she was - unpleasantly damp, moist, and wet
She knew now she had to release herself and take control
He, knowing her limitations because she had trusted him
With her most precious commodity her tender loving heart
He steps to the vase and pulls a rose from its place
He drops his guard and steps into her space
From her rear he kisses her gently on her neck
And placed the rose to her aching fragile heart
Passionately she turned, the rose was crushed
Between two burning hearts

Eye-Full

Was it the innocence?
Was it the radiance that emits from the emollient skin?
I tried to exonerate this turbid thought,
But I was deeply possessed by the aesthetics of some
unknown troll
Eyeful, eyeful
Was it the diamond cut shape of the eyes?
Was it the neatly razor curved eyebrows?
Was it the lengthy manicured eye-lashes?
Was it the smooth delicate cream that accents the eye-lids?
Suddenly, I closed my eyes to extricate this unknown troll
Eyeful, eyeful
Was it the straight structured outlines of the nose?
Was it the small beads of moisture that capture the covering
of the nostrils?
Was it the hot steaming exhalation that escapes the nose?
I briefly shifted my glance to egress my turbid thoughts
But there was no escape from this unknown troll
Eyeful, eyeful
Was it the particles of rays that illume the diamond studs that
graced the earlobes?
Was it the sharp distinctive vain lines that sculptured the ear?
I blink my eyes to ease myself from the candescent
But there was no escape from the unknown troll
Eyeful, eyeful
Was it the bi-flesh fold texture of the lips
Was it the oval opening of the mouth?
Was it the waxy subdued color on the lips
Openly I exhaled
I looked her capapie
I acknowledged her with a smile
She turned her eyes
Tenderly veiled her innocent, radiant emollient face with a tulle
She gently, quietly egressed my presence

Troll, supernatural being
Eyeful, eyeful

Dreams

What are dreams?
Idle time lost in subconsciousness
Moments of countless daze
Gently slipping away from reality
Into some unknown hemisphere
The instant can be vague and unclear
Moreover, real as a standing picture
You may be confronted with demons from the past
Or encounter moments of pleasant thoughts
You never know when and where
Dreams will take you
Unfortunately, it hadn't been planned
Dreams are feelings, thoughts or images
Experienced during sleep times
Lost in thoughts, hoping to achieve
Dreams can be terrifying shrinking you into fear
They can be inspiring, mingled with awe
Many people believe in dreams
While others never give thoughts
It is considered wasteless moments
Lost in a land with trolls
How many times I have nightmares
Sweaty, screaming out loud
Dreams can take you to various countries
Without ever leaving home
Dreams are visionary creations of imagination
A state of mind etched with abstracts
Suspending your thoughts from reality
When I need the impossible
All I do is dream, dream, dream
I had a dream, everything was delightful,

peaceful, quiet, and soothing
It was so pleasing, I knew I was in never, never land
Hope with faith, sometimes dreams come through

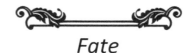

Fate

*T*wo people miles and miles away
Anticipate not what tomorrow brings
Or the perception of what lies ahead
By fate they crossed border lines
Into each other's path
With a stare of the eyes
Then politely, a gentle hi
The filament suddenly fervent
Engendering heat waves
Sending magnetic forces
Magnetizing two strangers
Resisting in their propelling
force

But fate has a way to work
To unite strangers at odds together
One is consistently persuasive
The other is gullible and giving
Then without realizing
A mutual bond is formed
Intimate association, affection, with esteem
They become inseparable
Trotting each other's path
Sharing each other's thoughts, trusting and confiding
Congenial, delectation to each other's likings
A genuine friendship has evolved
Between two people miles and miles away
They might say it's luck, destiny, even chance
Fate has it ways, it's inevitable

Feelings

*T*hat irresistible attribute that invades the body
Which penetrate the mind, soul, and the heart
That captures and ignites the fibers of the nerves
It enlightens you to a new persona of yourself with no
control
Which was unaware that it was hereditary
It cannot be bought, stolen, or sold
Or given to you by a friend, teacher, or parent
You have to search deep within to find
Then exhibit that emotion that mingles with passion
Then you realize that you have that latent attribute
that we all call feelings
It might exhibit itself in various modes
It might welt your eyes
But then, it might make the welted water flow
It's not unaware to make you cry
Then again it might just make you jitter
Shaking beyond control
But you never know, it might just let water
spring from your tiny pores
You have to bring it to a state of consciousness
in whatsoever you do
Which will reveal from the passion of that inner feeling>
Feelings...
So oftentimes we try to conceal our feelings
Hiding our emotions with pretense
Feelings are natural attributes that jitter the nerves
Feelings can be an emotional experience

A sensitivity to an intuitive understanding
A personal belief even with an opinion
Feelings can be an emotional state or reaction
Then again, it can be showing sensitivity to a situation
Feelings are the ability to show emotion
And the sensation to express sensitivity

Fire

I t emits a variant array of colors
It's hot, it's fierce, it's deadly
It burns, it disfigures, it kills
It is combustible
It is a paramount resource to our
lives
It provides an element of heat
Assisted to our daily task
It's a dependance
We rely on it flames to cook our
meals
It might be considered conflagration, greatly   destructive
But it has its good qualities
In sub temperatures it emits moderate heat,
to warm our dwelling place
In winter it adorns our fireplace
With a beautiful glow of radiant rays, and sparkling flames
It brings warmth to our home
Fire if it gets out of control
Can be destructive and will devastate
It has the ability to spread beyond control
It is intrepid - fearless
But h2o - water takes control
Yes, water dissipates fire
Water takes control
There is no more fire in control

Friendship

FINDING A GENUINE FRIEND IS SCARCE TO COME BY
BUT I FOUND A FRIEND WHEN I WAS LOST AND DESPAIRED
OH, WHAT FRIENDSHIP I HAVE COME TO KNOW
FRIENDSHIP IS LIKE A ROSE UNFOLDING ITS BEAUTIFUL PETALS
EXPOSING THE BEAUTY OF ITS SOUL
FRIENDSHIP IS GIVING YOURSELF BEYOND CONTROL
FRIENDSHIP IS A HEART OPEN WITH COMPASSION AND LOVE
FRIENDSHIP IS CARING WITHOUT A DOUBT
FRIENDSHIP IS GETTING TO KNOW AND UNDERSTAND THE ONE IN SHARING
FRIENDSHIP IS NO SECRETS UNTOLD
FRIENDSHIP IS BELIEVING IN THE ONE YOU HAVE COME TO KNOW
FRIENDSHIP IS A SINCERE BOND BETWEEN TWO SUBJECTS
FRIENDSHIP IS COMMITMENT IN SAME OF SPIRIT
FRIENDSHIP IS SUPPRESSING WHEN DOUBTS MIGHT ARISE
FRIENDSHIP IS MIRRORING EACH OTHER FAULTS
FRIENDSHIP IS SHARING IN GRIEF, HAPPINESS AND PAIN
FRIENDSHIP IS ABOUT RESPECT, PATIENCE AND HONESTY
OH WHAT FRIENDSHIP I HAVE COME TO KNOW
IN FRIENDSHIP THERE IS NO IMPATIENCE
IN FRIENDSHIP THERE IS A GLASS OF TRANSPARENCE
IN FRIENDSHIP THERE IS MOTIVATION WITHOUT ENVY
IN FRIENDSHIP THERE IS NO LEAVING OR FORSAKING
IN FRIENDSHIP THERE IS NO UNFAITHFULNESS
IN FRIENDSHIP THERE IS CONTINUOUS LOYALTY
FRIENDSHIP IS GIVING YOURSELF FREELY
FRIENDSHIP IS LOVE, CARING AND SACRIFICE
I HAVE FOUND A FRIEND, OH, SUCH A FRIEND
OH, WHAT FRIENDSHIP WE HAVE SHOWN
SUCH FRIENDSHIP WE HAVE COME TO KNOW AND SHARE

Hypocrites

*T*he world is full of hypocrites
    They pretend to be your friend
    But their hearts are against you
You read between, the lines of a hypocrite
It doesn't take long to discover a hypocrite
Though they come in disguise
The tell-tale signs are there all along
Their tongues are like two-edged swords
They change like the seasons
Never trust a hypocrite
There is no faith in their trust
Their words are not of value
Like genuine honest beings
Hypocrites are jealous people
With no mind of their own
They are full with envy
I despise every factor of a hypocrite
Hypocrites build strife
To satisfy their own egoistic selves
Hypocrites have no genuine friends
They don't know to be true to thine own self
Hypocrites are traitors, sell you out in a bit
Hypocrites are theatrical actors
They claim to be of a higher standard
But they are the biggest phonies
We all know a hypocrite
Are you a hypocrite? Don't take that road

Back To Mi Roots

It all begin pon the big iron bird
Air Jamaica the humming love bird
Flight to mi beautiful island
Di parish of Kingston well known as di ghetto
Mi disembark and mi stand a queue and stare way through
Mi have to be true, it was all new, but only fe a few
In comparison, mi receive all stare to mi disbelief
Mi wonder why all the stare
If mi nou in the land of mi true birth
The land that instill inna mi fe know the difference between right and wrong
Fe 'tan up fe wah yo believe in an' fight fe wah is fe yuh
Nou red eye fe other people commodity
God bless de child that's got im own
Se an' blind 'ear an' deaf, nou talk fe tell tales
Wi are a island with many colors, but outta many wi a one
But now mi know that them was true proverb of our old
Now mi look back and water drop out a mi eye When mi se the now guys
Them nou have nou pride for this beautiful island of sun shine
Yo never know the value of the vessel til the batty drop out
When mi open mi eye and se the wide open blue sea
Mi have retrospect of when mi was a pickny a dive with mi friends dem
Wi use to climb the people mango tree and kick ball in a di open field

Mi remember how mi use fe si dung and peel sugar cane with mi teeth like sharpen knife

Oh, what fun wi use to have with so much of little fe nam

From wi little in Jamaica wi instill with the fear of God

Yuh say yuh grace, yuh say yuh prayer, and fe sure wi have fe go to church

Oh, little island blessed with its own resource, how often time mi heart gripe for the land of mi birth

Beautiful, sweet, and precious Jamaica, land of wood and clear blue water

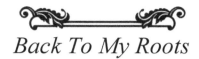

Back To My Roots

*I*t all began on the big iron bird
   Air Jamaica the humming love bird
   Straight flight to my beautiful island
The parish of Kingston, well known as the ghetto
I disembarked and I stand a queue and stare way through
I have to be true it was all new, but only to a few
In comparison I received all stares to my disbelief
I wondered why all the stares, if I was not
in the land of my true birth
The land that instilled in me to know the
difference between right and wrong
To stand up for what you believe in and
fight for what is yours
Don't red eyes for other people
commodity
God bless the child that's got his own
We are an island with many colors But,
out of many we are one
See and blind hear and deaf, no tell-tales
But now I know they were true proverbs
of our old
Now I look back and water flood my eyes
When I see the now guys
They don't have no pride for this beautiful island of sunshine
You never know the value of the vessel until the bottom falls out
When I open my eyes and see the wide-open blue sea
I have retrospect of when I was a child diving with my friends
We used to climb people's mango trees and kick ball in the open
field
Then I remember how I use to sit down and peel sugar cane with my
teeth like a sharpened knife
Oh, what fun we use to have with so much of little to eat

From we were little in Jamaica we were instilled with the fear of God

Did you say your grace? Did you say your prayers? And, for sure, we were in church

Oh, little island blessed with its own resources, how often times my heart gripes for the land of my birth

Beautiful, sweet, and precious Jamaica, land of wood and clear blue waters

HEAVEN

Heaven Oh Heaven
I cry so mush, for this Divine Heaven
Where is this, Heaven?
Some anticipate the sky as Heaven
It is high above the Earth
Ascend the high blue sky
Heaven is a beautiful creation
No agitation, composure in serenity and peacefulness
Impeccable - incapable of sin
No darkness in sight
Adorned with glows of soft crystal lights
Where the streets are mirrored gold like transparent glass
Serenades in celestial strings
Angels adorn between the cherubims
Giving praises, in unison, playing the Lord's harp
Invocation of Devine blessing
A bliss - perfect happiness
Lovely - Delightful - Beautiful - Devine
An elevation of the highest degree
There is no hedonism, there is no heathenism
One glorious day I will finally get to Heaven
His angels will escort me through Heaven's gate
There, I will sit with Abraham, Isaac, and Jacob
Where death is perpetually conquered, immorality lives forever
Oh yes, I am in Heaven

How Could It Be

*H*ow can it be?
  I stand in awe, returned to the land of my birth
  A land blessed with peace and love with foreseen hope
Understanding, I haven't, though I tried to comprehend
How could it be?
Am I so strangely different from my aboriginals
With such fear I hope not to see the dawning of the morning
I could not believe I was in the land of my nativity
The relapse of time could not cause such devastation to mankind
I mirrored myself to the comparison of my brothers and sisters
Not in physical countenance but even so there were understanding
differences
I saw a new world even though I still inhabited the same world
A painful sight my teary eyes beheld
The land was in disarray, blanket with mountainous refuse
Streams of limey green unfiltered waters
Rubbish in piles and piles unnoticed but in sight of the eyes
But while I pondered, the answer was realistically in full sight
Humanity has lost touch with the essence of reality
Individuals have dehumanized themselves with artificial exposure
l struggled wondering if there was a mass cloud
That overshadowed the eyes of the land
Has the desire for knowledge become naught?
Where are the self-thinkers? Is there no one to discern
between right and wrong, good and bad, weak and strong?
It was obvious that I could not solve the default of my people
I sadly observed a land of inhabitants divided in divisions of class
The unfortunate who possessed not and the privileged who have
So, for refuge and comfort in the land of my birth- I reminisced
Reflecting on the beauty around the land of God's natural creations

The Vital Map

*T*here is a map that lines our direction
　　It has crimson vibrant color, red as blood
　　Ever tracing its bright lines of direction
It embodies us to direct our ways
Lively, a unique shape of the heart
It never stops mapping new direction of our life
The directions are ever so right
Even so it confuses the mind
Since ancient time many depend on this heart shaped map
Unrealized, some avoid the significance of its daily direction
Lost in their journey of life
Opposed to adhere to rightful direction
Dependable is this map that's shaped as a heart
Its mapping lines might fade but never be broken
During years of facilitating our ways
Reliable we are on this map since our journey
It's not unusual for us to get lost in our direction

Just as the lines fade, our eyes fail
Our minds drift off the road we travelled so frequently
How fortunate and loved we are, having an indwelling map
A map to correct our wrong direction of decisions
Many chose not to obey the indelible lines of direction
Proud in their own ego, blind in their stubbornness
There is an open abyss unavoidable in wait
Obey not the lines? fail to adhere correction?
Follow the heart shaped map, obey its direction
It provides the perfect instruction
Behold, open your eyes, follow your heart in the right direction

Who Am I?

*W*ho am I ?
　　A gentle touch with caring hands
　　A tender heart, a flowing spring of charity
A voice crying out, full with directions
How many times I have lost my path
Story telling in the dark of my mind
Confused to find rays of light
Darkness, it's not right
Oh fog, why do you daunt my mind?
Why do you laugh at me
Life is not a joke to strive in this land
In the tunnel of fun fear takes control
Who am I?
Seasons of the time, shades of colors
My spirit is as the brown Autumn leaves
Overshadowed in every open space
As the chlorophyll debilitates, so is my energy
Rustic autumn is like the swing of my moods
Old white snowy winter blessed with ancient festivity
Is there any reason my beard is as pale as white?
Seasons change reflecting diverse colors
Producing Variant kinds of mood swings
Confusing spring, confused just as my mind
I am confused just as the seasons of time
My mood transforms to reflect days of the seasons
Happy Friday, Joyous Sunday, Blue Monday
Harvest time when fruits are on the vine
On occasions I am blessed with increase beyond
Snow, rain, mixed with cold,
Why don't you make up your mind
Who am I?
The gift of the earth for His set time
I am nature the elements of life

Silver, gold, chromium these are just a few
Hidden traces of life's essentials
I am fossil strong as the ancient rocks
The glittering lights from granite
Time travels, so do the thoughts of my mind
Who am I?
I am an animate spot in the space of time

SEA

*W*aves of mystical blue water
    Blue skies transcend clear water into azure
    Body of limitless measurement of water
Vastest of water to the end of the earth
The ocean emits sounds of wails and groans
Rhythms of the ocean in fierce force
Building tsunami tidal waves with perilous force
laboring through its waves, silencing on shore
In the midst of water eyes marveled
While the ship slowly tries to haste away
Sea with depth of water, precious things beneath
Deep and wide with living creatures
Imagine, postcards that eyes will never see
large and small fishes, numerous marine species
The sea, a habitation for a large population
The ocean, a nation of various organisms
Animals, plants, single celled life forms
They all are whole with independent life
Human eyes never saw and will never see
An abyss of a subaquatic garden
Beautiful coralline formations form colorful corals
Sea weeds, large reefs, a vein of colorful ore
Corals, hard stony substances of external skeletons
Deep beneath there lies a university of marine biology
The sea, a universe without borders

Flowing fort, an international pathway
Man has created wonders of the sea, such as the Panama Canal
Ships, boats, and barge sails the high sea
Transforming a body of water into a busy highway
Sailors navigating exhibiting their nautical experiences
In spots, small acres of dry grounds inhabit on water
Islands of many sizes evolves in various spaces
Limed mountains stand tall projecting through blue waters
Forms islands spectacular for eyes to see and thoughts to wonder
Parcels of land with green vegetation, boated to and from
Sea, the vast expanse of salt water,
Question, where does the salt come from?
Why does the sea water fixate with salt?
Take a peek beneath at the clear water
And you will see far as your eyes can focus
Water full with reflections, a sea of faces
Tranquil, floating on a body of cascading waves of water

HOME

I long for *home*
I wonder about *home*
I miss *home*
Where is *home*?
Home is my dwelling place
Home is where I seek refuge
Home is where I can be mirrored
Home is where I exhibit the true me
Home is where we instill pride and character
in our children
Home is where we adopt family values
Home is where I interact with my love ones
Home is where we sit in unity and bless our meals
Home is where I lay my head each night and dream
sweet dreams
Home is where we arise each morning and embrace each other with
anew morning of love
Home is where I have delectation
Home is where I give invitation to peace and quietness
Home is where the heart is
Home is where I recumbent and reflect
My *home* is habitable
My *home* is not elegantly decorated
My *home* is just simple- *homely*
Delightful, lovely, and beautiful
I am glad to be *home*

FACES

*F**ace, visage, countenance a person's frontal***
  Beautiful stranger, a face I saw like sunlight from a far
  A face as an angel, unexpectedly I met
A face that transcends happiness
A face that reflects feelings when I look into the eyes
Out of the many faces I get to see that faces are unique
Appearances, no two faces are the same
From the head, forehead, to the individual chin
Each person's face expresses their own personality
The mouth, the ears, the eyes and the nose
The joining corresponding parts of the face
How often times we know
That faces sometimes don't tell the truth

Silently expressing a face full with deception
Faces expose the understatement of their experience
Pain, sorrow, joy, happiness, even defeat
Moody face, sad face, happy face
What's up with that sour face?
The speechless unacceptable faces
What about the face off with attitude of confrontation?
Many faces surface superficial smiles
How truthful, faces are a visible reflection of the invisible soul
The inner transformation reflects the face
An angry word from the mouth, a sly glance from the face
May reveal a miserable soul
Kind eyes with a gentle look, a warm welcoming smile
Transform the mask of a healthy and happy soul
Surely, we can't do anything about the face we inherit
But let us transfer our invisible soul onto our visible face
Exhibiting a happy face with a welcoming hospitable smile

Wild Flower

Trotting on a large open field
Footing through human made tracks
On land fully cultivated but not by man's hand
I was in the midst of various plants
As common as they were, their names I knew not
My briskly steps lose their momentum
My eyes realized they have one thing in common
The plants were all budded in variance of colors
In the multitude of my thoughts, I ponder
My thought took me deep in wonder
Complex in awe, I fixed my eyes
How awesome is the omnipotent Spirit?
I saw His goodness in the land of waste
Springtime and beauty were on the waste land
Each wild shrub interlocked in a network of flowers
Preoccupied and obsessed I was with nature's art
On a blanket of fresh green grass were an array of colors
Wild flowers growing uncontrollably
Unrestrained in its natural environment
Shrubbery of wild flowers were on display
Tinny spots of multiple colors stand on small stems
Implanted between branches of green leaves
Red, yellow, lavender, pink, oh, how can I forget white

Wild flowers in bloom spread across acres of waste land
There they were, doing their ritual on the trees
I watched the birds and the bees hopping on the trees
I wondered, do they enjoy the joy of beauty
Such a blending was even more beautiful
Wild flowers are beautiful as any other flowers
They just grow in the wild, they are God's creation
The creator is a Spirit of beauty
Wild flowers spectacular on stems hides in greens
Wild flowers mixed with weeds waving silently in the breeze
Strangely in life's seasons I tread the grounds
There were no wild flowers waving in the silent breeze
Autumn wind blows over wild flowers
Wild flowers are latent in their places

I FELT YOUR PAIN

Give me your eyes
I will regenerate
Your vision to see once again
The beauty of life

ذتپتذ

Yield me your ears
I will enchant you
With decibel of harmonic peal
I will let you hear once again
The birds singing against
the windowpanes

ذتتذ

Surrender me your mouth
I will restructure your vocal cord
You will once again pronounce
your vowels with eloquence

ذتپتذ

Trade me your feet
I will walk your weary
and tiresome journey
In slow strides to places
You once trotted

ذثتث

Put fort your hands in my hands
I will lead you to that quiet
Place of serenity
Where you sit and reminisce nostalgic
On the life you once knew
The vigor and strength of youth
The burning passion of intimacy
The ever-given friendship
The close knitted family ties
Now - have your rest
I felt your pain

ذثتث

The Tongue

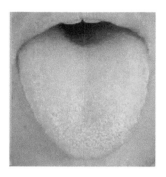

The tongue
A small muscular organ that equipped the mouth
Covered with moist mucosa, tiny papillae
It's known for its unpredictable characteristics
The tongue shaped like a miniature sword
Little and concealed in the mouth
Guarded and protected by a door of two lips
It is filled with diversion, it cannot be trusted
You will find out that it is a traitor
When it finally betrays you
It respects no man, prejudiced, it's not
It defends and offends with the hiss of the teeth
It stings like a serpent with poisonous venom
It blesses and curses, it is a two-edged sword
A slip of the tongue can cause great damage
Ignites a fire and spread like wildfire
With its slandering gossip and tell-tales
Undoubtable condemning innocent people's life
One wrong word of the tongue can ruin one's reputation
The tongue is toxic, it is a poisonous, restless weapon
It can cause great harm with its evil report
The tongue is a difficult task to contain or tame
No one can tame the tongue from its natural abilities

It has the power to build up and tear down
The tongue boasts boisterously
Man tames the animals but he cannot tame the tongue
The tongue is an unruly member of the body
Out of the mouth proceeds good and bad, hatred and love
Let's muzzle our mouths and keep our tongues from speaking evil
Let's keep our lips from lies, let's strive in upright conversations

The Virtue Woman

Is there a virtue woman?
Who is this virtue woman?
It's hard to find such a woman
Of such unique characteristics
She is a peculiar woman
Distinguishes herself from her peers
With the perfect attributes
That makes any man care
She is peaceful and loving
She gives of herself abundantly
Not expecting any rewards
Her inner strength is unbelievable
It is unimaginable to the eyes
She is different from the rest
She is poise to do, with pride and dignity
Blessed with wisdom and understanding
She is committed to her family
So, she holds them most dear
In her heart is kindness
She cares not about vain beauty
She is graceful in her steps
There is no idle path in her day
Many feign to be virtuous
But she excels them all
she has well been counted worthy of honor
She is worthy of all honors

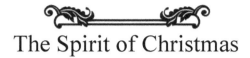

The Spirit of Christmas

I was amused in a child's mind, icicle frozen was the windowpane
Glistened ice were the hanging tapering pieces of freezing dripping water
My eyes, I strained looking through the frosted windowpane
The stars were sparkling through the dark atmosphere
The halo lights in the heavens were like ice crystals
I remember there were lights reflecting from the falling wet white snow
During the stillness of my mind reflecting on the beauty that was before my eyes
My hearing was in tune with old familiar songs learned as a child
Strangely, I began to reminisce, my mind was deeply indulged
How could I remember so transparently from a child
Amazed and excited I was, drifting back in time
I smiled and I laughed, it was just like yesterday once again
I waited and anticipated what surprises were in store
Drinking hot chocolate mingled with peppermint candy sticks
While in bed watching the big snowflakes falling from the sky
It was after dark, amazingly, I can see everything clearly
Evergreens fully dressed in glittering snow
Emitting nose catching scents of fragrant holiday pine
Fireplace glowing amber flames, popping flying tiny sparks
Mom and pop sitting closely sipping spicy eggnog
Carols resounding jollying the hearts, inspiring to sing along
Silent night, holy night, all is bright, all is in light, surround the peaceful night
The dawn of Christmas had arrived, Santa Clause was in sight
I was still amazed with smiles, happy and joyous still as a child
Those are the things we will always remember at Christmas time

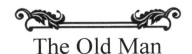

The Old Man

H appy couples stroll by
Savoring the moonlight glow
Unreluctantly, they gazed at the old man
Strangely, about the lonely old man
He knew all about walking hand in hand
Chasing the moonlight, wishing on a falling star
Love is strange as tomorrow
Finds foot notes of yesterday
Moments change and so does the heart
He will treasure the void in his heart
While he continues to chase the moon and the stars
Hoping to wish on a falling star
He watches the bird stand alone on a single fence post
Realized he, that he is no different
From a dove mourning for love
Lonely he remains reminiscing whispered words of love
Unrealized, that his eyes boil tears
While his eyelids gush out water
Creation has it seasons
Love is strange rotating through its season
Realized he then, that loneliness is self- illusion
How can he be lonely when he has breath
Breathing the sources of life

Dwelling in a world clustered with lively vegetation
Domestic animals that are delightful to pat
Flying creatures that stop by time to time
With sweet lyrics that sounds like lullabies
He glances around and proclaims, "nature is beautiful"
Nature is in her beauty, in her blanket of white
Winter is nigh, icicles and frosty needle pines
Seasons come and seasons go
How much longer will I go?
I hope to catch one more falling star
Life is full of odd surprises
I have seen more than a few in my time
Life has also thrown its various demands
But no surprise, He always provides

Summer Pleasure

L et the opulent, ruminate caviar and crab cakes
Some are more delightfully indulged in soft
shell crabs and scrumptious lobster tails
Sipping steamy New England clam chowder
Escaping the sweltering summer heat
In sleek dingy outdoor pavilions
Somewhere out there
In the midst of old country Maine
Digesting the sultry ocean
On a hazy summer day
Where the low torrid sun
Embraced the wide-open seas
Emitting mosaic rays
Beneath its fervid heat waves
Where the ocean breeze
Interludes the warmth atmosphere
Over the calm blue seas
Waiting to quench your hot steaming fate
Where summer pleasures begin to mate
Where birds make canopy over the
wide open beach
Where children become sun gods
Merry making with sand pales
Gathering all, but little seashells
Along the parched seashore

Stillness

I felt the gentle wind whirling uninterrupted
It was cool, refreshing to my spirit
It's not unusual to hear the sound of the wind
Not having sight of its approach
The fluttering wings of the birds I heard
Surely, with sweet harmonic sounds to my ears
But strangely their direction was not beheld
There were no birds in sight
The gentle flow of stimulating water I heard
Rushing its way against the buried rocks
Which gave calm to my tired soul
My hand, I reached to grope the peaceful water
But strangely with much curiosity there was naught
Then I realized, the wind was stilled
There were no flying birds in the air
The calm stream was dried ground
In an imaginary state I was
All my sorrow and sighing had fled
Experiencing I, my desire
The calmness of peace and tranquility

Smoke

It drifts and drifts and be drifts
  In slow steady fluent motion
    Across its wide-open space
In its travel it never goes down
It accents up, side way or in-between
At times the invisible wind
Control its visible directions
It might emit multicolor
Grey, black, or white
You never see fire without one of its colors
Smokey Joe tries to prevent many wildfires
It exhausts through the chimney
And try to escape through the fire

One puff, two puffs, three puffs
Exhaling the human nostril
I watched it escape the flue
Where it dissipated in the open atmosphere
You have seen it often times
Watching the ships on their voyage
How many times you have seen it as a cloud of fog?
Bewildered, I watched the visible gas
Escaping from a burning substance
It was a column of a cloudy mass of smoke
Inevitable I was inhaling a mass of poisoned fume
Let's be aware smoke can be harmful
Not to forget, devastatingly deadly
Through burning eyes, I looked to the hill
I saw a mass of smoke candescent
Across the dark and cloudy sky

TEARS

Sweet tears, bitter tears
There are all streams of emotional plight
Tears evolve from anger and pain
That built up inside and stored
Uncontrollable from the high point of stress
The tears will spontaneously erupt
Unable to sustain the pressure at hand
The tears inundate the heart to its content
Chasing after empty treasure
Only will break your heart
Which always bring tears
To comfort the broken heart
But tears will not always satisfy
The discomfort of hearts
We must find fulfilment in the soul
To keep us emotionally strong
Soon you find there are no more tears
That freely shed along
The power and strength of courage
Dormant will the tears that cried
But many a tear of to fall
Because it's all in the game of emotions
Find the courage to laugh
Even though your heart is aching.

THE Cyprian

She was innocent
Beauty beyond imagination
Lived all her life mandated
With strict supervision
Blessed with all the essential things in life
Friends to share deep thoughts
Parents to protect her from the wrath of life
She was happy and full of life
Cynosure – always in the center of attraction
Gracious to the young men that came in her sight
Attention she always sought
Undressing in nudity is all she ever knew
Exposing her nakedness like picture shows
Revealing her most sacred body parts
Disrespecting herself with no regard
Walking the unprotective streets from dust, till dawn
Looking for johns, turning her tricks, in and out
Haven't given consideration to what the outcomes might be
Is it for the monetary reward? is it the want for affection?
It can't be the want for love
Love is feeling, love is expressions from the heart
My daughter, my womb
I should have remained barren
Your sacred body is more valuable than the priceless pearls
Why are you playing the harlot, the lady of the night
Where is the virtuous woman?

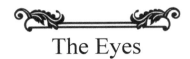

The Eyes

The eyes are the smallest member of the body
The organ that produces sight
The eyes are small, they are deep
They have their own unique shape
Accentuate with variance of colors
some earth brown, some pretty blue
Peeping from their protective lids
The eyes can become fiery red
Or teary wet from tiresome stress
The eyes beam us to the light
Give one the eye and they will draw their own conclusion
An eye for an eye, I have my eyes on you
I closed my eyes, refused to acknowledge what's in sight
Through the eyes we view the beauties of creation
The eyes guide our steps to and fro
What would life be without the eyes?
A still cloud of darkness, bolted
The eyes do not deceive, the heart does
During antiquity they may lose their shape
Become weak and frail
But it has left us with beautiful memories
It has swollen at times with stares
Light and darkness unfolds
We never know when and what the eyes will see

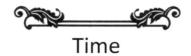

Time

Tick Tock, Tick Tock, Tick Tock
It's all an accumulation of time
A second, a minute, an hour
The clock is chiming by
The clock, a vital instrument of time
Years come years go - bye
In times, sorrow, grief and pain
In times, laughter, gladness and joy
What is this life?
Our life is recorded by time
Time is essence
Time is virtue
Time is paramount
Where is all the time?

Strangely it might seem, but true
Time passes on with the blink of an eye
What do we know about time?
Time is infinite but there is never much time
We have no time to stand and stare
With all fairness, time is not prejudice
Time waits on no man
Time is nowhere in sight

SKY

There, I stood stilled
Bewildered in a daze
Was I here? In the presence
of some strange unknown place?
Suddenly my eyes, my mind,
with my divided thoughts, evolved
There I saw the thick clustered gray clouds
Coalesced and floating
Across the high and global blue sky
The forceful wind blew much out of control
Suddenly there was darkness all around
The leaves flew like birds
Losing their momentum
leaving a foliage on the ground
Was it the clouds in motion?
Or is it the coalescent vapor that
gently floating in the sky?
There I stood stilled, bewildered in a daze
There I saw the gentle clustered clouds
Evanescent from the high sky
There I stood, evoked
Then I saw no gray or white clouds in the sky
All I saw was Nature's high and yawning blue sky
Not even the sun, the moon or the stars were in sight
Only Nature's high and wide blue sky.

The Power of Love

Love is like fire
Emits the most vehement flame
Love has no borders or standards
Love defaults your every conscious thought
Love empowers the heart and weakens the mind
Love takes control and get its way
Love is as able, powerful as death
Love manipulates your mind and confuses the heart
Love is gentle and tender but beware
Love tears the heart and turns man into a beast
Why then harbor jealousy which is cruel as the grave
Love transcends all my feelings
Am I in control of my mental faculty?
All the waters cannot quench my love
Neither can the floods drown its flame
It burns within like an uncontrolled hearth
Love festers the heart, the mind,
and the soul
Love is a flaming fire
love is an awesome feeling of
desire
Love emits the soul with joy and
peace
May find its way any moment
unexpectedly
Love is the greatest feeling - find
yourself in love
If I give all the treasures of my
house - for love
Surely - it would be contentment
Let bind a seal upon our hearts
And seal them with a burning - fiery kiss

"I love you"

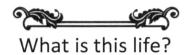

What is this life?

What is this life?
Wipe the tears from my eyes
I am blind from corruption
Greed, injustice, immorality
The unrighteousness of mankind
            I
What is this life?
Life is a mystery
Presumptuously, I try to understand
The complexity of life
But it's a maze that baffles the brain
Man's doings are of self-intent
So how can one understand his ways
His ways are right in his own eyes
It's an unending, unpredictable mystery
Of the unrighteousness of mankind
            T
What is this life?
Life is the perfect gift
We are born in a confused world
Confusion invades the mind
To the unrighteousness of mankind
We are in a deep slumber
Let us awake from the destruction
Of mankind's unrighteousness
            L
What is this life?
Diversification >>>
Where there is peace, Love and harmony
The understanding of each being
Reflections of the inner beauty
The true righteousness of mankind
What is this life?

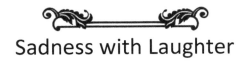

Sadness with Laughter

I laugh because I am happy
But strangely I even laugh when I am sad
Laughter soothes the pains that often makes me cry
I find solace and joy from the tears I cry
Tears are antidote for sadness deep inside
But laughter is medicine that shields the eyes from tears
When I laugh, I get the pleasure from nature's melody
Sweet laughter defeats the unhappy spell
Sadness and happiness infused tears and laughter
Tears of sadness twinkle into laughter of joy
Sweet, bitter moments, life is unpredictable
One moment is happiness and laughter
Next moment is sadness and tears
But most definitely, laughter always prevails
Laughter soothes the soul and uplifts the spirit
Laughter symbolizes the spirit of happiness
Remember the next time you feel the pain of sadness
Find the courage to reach deep inside
Then laugh instead of cry.

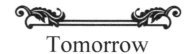

Tomorrow

T omorrow, we look forward to embrace
Unfortunately, a day of no assurance
A person, tomorrow owes no promise
Indulge in today that you both have greeted
Why wait until tomorrow to share your most intimate thoughts
Tomorrow hasn't promised you breath, with sunlight to see
Don't blame tomorrow for not achieving your desire
You had the opportunity you should have grasped today
What have you got from today's promises?
Appreciate and enjoy it while having it
Smile and make hay while the sun shines
Continue to capture nature's beauty in the light of today
Tomorrow may never come to savor its work of art

Optimistic, we can't depend on tomorrow to rejoice in His creation
Pessimistic, we can't misuse today, perceiving tomorrow's desire
Live your dreams today, tomorrow may never enlighten its reality
Make the best of today, observe, meditate and rejoice
Tomorrow may rob your thought of the chance to recapture yesterday
Keep thinking about the unfinished today that rolls into tomorrow
Why perceived tomorrow, not yet in its presence
Your perception- tomorrow will produce happiness
Pause- today happiness is here, always at present
Dismiss your principles of restriction and enjoy life
Complete your daily tasks today disregarding tomorrow
Live the presence of today and dismiss your illusion of tomorrow
Yesterday spent, left and went beyond yonder
Today is nigh at hand, tomorrow sits contemporaneously
Thanks for yesterday that edified me

Thanks for today that I may learn from my yesterday
If tomorrow comes, I hope to surpass
In the light of today- find hope in the Lord
Your tomorrow may be darkness
Let's give God thanks for the completion of today
And let's pray for the sunlight of tomorrow

About the Author

It seems like yesterday, but in the factual life of reality, it's been years... perhaps even a decade. As I meditated and focused on relaxing that morning, as I did every day before work, I sat to read the daily newspaper. The time period was some month in the year 1998. I read an article in the newspaper which was really a contest publication seeking amateur poets. I stopped to ponder if I was truly worthy enough to write a poem? I answered my question at the moment, formulating beautiful words into sentences. Surprisingly, that same day I finished my first poem called *Beauty Creation*.

In need of satisfying my confidence of my curiosity, I called my son who was out of the state, attending college, I read *'Beauty Creation'* into his listening ears.

He inquired, "Who is the poet that penned such a natural observation."

Stunned by his question, I laughed, then announced, "I wrote it."

He laughed and replied, "No dad, you did not write that beautiful poem." He was finally convinced when my daughter took the phone and explained to him that she typed the handwritten words.

Out of curiosity, I entered the contest submitting my poem, *'Beauty Creation'*. Sometime passed when one day I received a letter. Enclosed within it, there was a certificate bearing my name as "Poet of the Year". Ever since that day, I never stopped expressing my artistic creations, forming words into beautiful sentences with meaning for readers to perceive and digest.

Beauty Creation is my first poem. I wrote my first book of poems with its presence making it take initiative at the preface in the book.

Who am I?

I would imagine the poem *'Beauty Creation'* personify me in some effectual attribute of mental faculties of my perception and geniality. I love and admire beauty and its presence in nature. Nature of the creation of the Supreme God refreshes me with peace. I strive to obtain knowledge, seeking wisdom, hoping to understand. I respect others with expectation of reward in the same manner. I live my life on the foundation of integrity, not with false balance but evenly with a just weight. Honesty, love and truth, character traits that delight my spirit. I consider that I am a humble and lowly person blessed with happiness and love. I am satisfied with what life has made accessible to me - with profound thanks.

I am fortunate, considering that I am retired for quite some years and seeing myself in excellent health, with lengthened time that allows me to go after my passion to reminisce about happy moments, satisfying my desire of variance of beauty in different countries of the world. I have had the privilege and pleasure to attain the sights of six continents of the seven great and beautiful divisions of the countries of the globe. Visiting the many countries, I had the opportunity to see between the lines, a wide perspective of human's nature.

Lightning Source UK Ltd.
Milton Keynes UK
UKHW051448120223
416624UK00009B/27

9 798986 296210